# The Princes of Hastinapur

Subhadra Sen Gupta

**Om Books International**

After the sons of Vichitravirya grew up, Pandu became the king of Hastinapur. He was married twice; first to Kunti, the princess of Mathura and then to Madri the princess of Madra. Dhritarashtra was married to Gandhari, the daughter of the king of Gandhara.

When Gandhari found out that her husband Dhritarashtra was blind, she decided to cover her eyes for the rest of her life and not see the world, like her husband. This made her brother Shakuni very angry and he vowed to take revenge on the Kuru family of Hastinapur one day.

One day, when King Pandu was out in the forest hunting, he heard a sound behind a bush and thinking it was a wild deer, he aimed his arrow towards the sound. He hit Sage Kindama, who before dying cursed Pandu. A deeply saddened Pandu decided to retire to the forest with his wives Kunti and Madri.

Dhritarashtra now became the king of Hastinapur in spite of his blindness. He, and his queen, Gandhari, had a hundred sons. They named the eldest Duryodhana and the second son, Dusshasana. The eldest among the Hastinapur princes was Pandu and Kunti's son, Yudhishthira.

When Pandu's senior queen Kunti was a young girl in Mathura, Sage Durvasa had come to visit her father's palace. Her father said to her, "Child, serve Sage Durvasa well. He becomes angry very quickly and I don't want him to curse us."

So Kunti served the sage with a lot of care and respect and he was very pleased with her. While leaving, he blessed Kunti and granted her a special boon.

Durvasa said, “Kunti, I will teach you a very special mantra. With this mantra you will become the mother of sons who will be great warriors. But be careful when you chant it! Because by this mantra you can summon any of our gods who will give you a son.”

Kunti was delighted with the boon. She thought, "I can summon any god and they will give me sons!" Then she became curious and wondered, "Will the boon really work?"

So Kunti looked up to the sky where Surya, the Sun God was glowing. She prayed to him saying, "Surya, give me a son." And to her surprise her prayers were answered!

Young Kunti gave birth to a son. The boy wore the armour of the Sun God.

Afraid to tell her father, Kunti thought anxiously, Oh what do I do?" In desperation, she put the baby in a basket and floated it away on the River Yamuna. She stood there weeping as she watched the basket float away, praying that her son would be safe.

Kunti's prayers were answered. The basket was found by a charioteer named Adhiratha and his wife Radha, who did not have any children. Radha picked up the baby and cried out in delight, "Our prayers have been answered. The gods have given us a son!" They named the baby, Karna.

Kunti and Madri were very sad as they did not have any children. Then Kunti remembered the boon given by Sage Durvasa. She prayed to Dharma, the God of Justice, and her eldest son Yudhishthira was born.

Wind God Vayu, gifted her the second son named Bhima. Indra, the Lord of the Heavens, became the father of her third son, Arjuna. Each son possessed the divine powers of his father.

Madri prayed to the twin gods of the morning and evening stars called Ashwins and she had twin sons, who were named Nakul and Sahadev. When both King Pandu and Queen Madri died suddenly, Kunti decided to return to Hastinapur with the five children.